A
Winning
Attitude

— ❖ ❖ ❖ ❖ ❖ ❖ ❖ —

A
Winning
Attitude

— ❖ ❖ ❖ ❖ ❖ ❖ ❖ —

How to Develop Your Most Important Asset

by Michelle Fairfield Poley

SkillPath Publications
Mission, KS

Editor
Kelly Scanlon

Cover Design
Rod Hankins

Illustrations
Diane Flynn and Pauline Hayes

Library of Congress Catalog Card Number: 95-71730

ISBN: 978-1-878542-28-1

Printed in the United States of America

Contents

*Dedicated with love to
Ross, Eleanor, and Michael Poley,
Nola Herman and Denise Dudley.
They are the best family an author could have.*

*Also to Mark Addy.
His attitude sets an example for us all.*

Preface

Working with yourself to develop a positive, winning attitude is the most rewarding work you can do.

When you improve your outlook on life, every area of your life improves.

You see, your attitude is the mental device that filters reality for you. It doesn't matter whether that reality has to do with your career, your relationships, your inner self or even your finances. It is your attitude that tells you what you believe about the people, places, things and events of your life.

Experts in the field of human potential tell us that the things we believe about ourselves and our lives tend to come true. If we believe we are failures, we generally become failures. If we believe we are winners, we become winners.

This book will foster in you the habit of thinking well of yourself and of the people, places, things and events in your world. And that is, indeed, the first, most important step you can take toward reaching your goals and fulfilling your dreams.

Please keep an open mind as you read the following pages. TRY the exercises and suggestions presented. If you are hoping to receive the full benefit of this book, you will need to tread some new ground. If you always do what you always did, you'll always get what you always got. This means that in order to change, you must do some new things—you must take some chances.

I am convinced that attitude is the single most important thing an individual possesses. In my career as a training consultant, I have met thousands of people across the United States. Some have faced incredible challenges in their lives and have appeared to be beaten down by them. Others who have faced those same challenges have turned them into advantages by refusing to give up.

Don't ever give up. You have the ability to make life exactly what you want it to be. It's all in your attitude.

Best wishes to you as you embark on the road to success!

Michelle Fairfield Poley

PART ONE

Attitudes
Have Outcomes

▬

Read the title of this section again: Attitudes Have Outcomes. Remember that as you read through the following situations and as you progress through this book.

Sandy knew from Day One at her new job that she'd made a terrible mistake. Her boss, Mr. Taylor, was a tyrant!

He scowled at her every time he walked by her desk, and it was already clear that he was a nit-picking perfectionist. Well, Sandy simply wouldn't tolerate it. If he was going to treat her that way, she was not going to go out of her way to do a good job. Obviously, she'd never be able to make him happy.

He would just have to learn that he was being unreasonable.

Cara's new job was a real challenge. She'd never worked for such a goal-oriented boss before. This man never let up! Every minute of his day (and Cara's) was filled with activity. Cara realized right away that to be a success in this job, her work habits were going to have to change dramatically. She was used to a slower pace.

But, she figured, the change would be good for her. It would stretch her abilities and help her forget her upcoming divorce, maybe even help her learn some new skills and improve her chances for getting into management someday.

"Oh well," she laughed to herself, "I'd better start eating a high-protein breakfast!"

Sandy had taken her job as Mr. Taylor's administrative assistant on May 15. Three months later, after four warnings to improve her attitude, she was replaced by a new administrative assistant—Cara.

By the end of that year, Sandy had held three other jobs, but none of them for more than six weeks. Also by the end of that year, Cara was replaced—so she could take on her new position in the company: sales manager.

Mr. Taylor had been impressed with Cara's willingness to accept responsibility and her enthusiasm for difficult projects. He figured that she was just the shot in the arm the company's lagging sales needed.

Cara's promotion brought with it a salary increase of $6,000 a year.

———————— ❖ ————————

Robert led a very comfortable life. His house was well-kept, his clothes were always impeccably pressed, his exercise program and diet kept him lean and strong, and his outstanding gift for organizing made him the top computer programmer in his organization.

When he met Sara, he could tell it was the beginning of something wonderful. They dated two evenings a week and spent all day together every Sunday. Robert especially enjoyed playing with Sara's five-year-old daughter, Maria. After a couple of years, Sara and Robert married and Sara and Maria moved into his house.

Within a week, Robert was wondering whether he'd made a mistake. Maria was having a hard time sleeping in a new place, and he and Sara were up half the night with her. That made it difficult for Robert to wake up early enough to work out, and if he didn't work out, he felt his whole day was out of kilter.

It was true that Robert took great care of himself; he had organized his life to do just that. He was dismayed by how much these two other people had disrupted his schedule. Everything had worked so well before they moved in!

Within a year, Robert and Sara were divorced. The house seemed a little too quiet, and Robert had to admit he felt pretty lonely. But at least he was back to his routine!

Drew was Robert's brother. He, too, had recently married a woman with a daughter. Mary Ellen was a great wife, and he figured having three-year-old Sadie around was just the thing to keep him from taking his fortieth birthday too seriously.

Sure, sometimes it was hard to get out of bed in the morning after being up half the night when Sadie was too excited to sleep. But, he thought, there were a few years in the not-too-distant past that he had spent worrying that he'd never get to be a father. It seemed to him that he should count his blessings.

Joe was diagnosed with multiple sclerosis the day after his thirtieth birthday, just four months after his promotion to personnel director. He was the youngest person ever to hold that position in his company, and he was quite proud of the accomplishment. "It just isn't fair," he thought. "Why me? Right when I was getting ahead in my life."

He called his wife from the doctor's office: "Honey, I'm going to need a wheelchair." He stated the news matter-of-factly.

He took the rest of the day off and composed his letter of resignation. He was sure he would be unable to perform his job duties from a wheelchair, so he decided he might as well get the resignation over with.

The next morning, he met with his boss and explained the situation. His boss expressed sympathy and urged Joe to stay on.

He didn't understand Joe's insistence that he wouldn't be able to do the job.

On the other end of the country, Jack was diagnosed with the same disease. His doctor explained the usual progression of the illness.

Jack called his wife. "I don't know, " he said. "I just can't imagine myself in a wheelchair."

Jack went to the library and studied about MS. He requested medical journals from the university and found many articles about progressive treatments. By the end of the month, he was on a vegetarian diet, seeing a chiropractor twice a week, working with a hypnotist and looking into acupuncturists in the area.

The contacts he made as he tried everything in his power to remain healthy eventually led him to a support group of others diagnosed with MS. The goal of their meetings was to help each other stay totally and completely healthy by sharing information and support.

After resigning as personnel director of his company, Joe filed for disability with the state. Three months later, as he had predicted, he was in a wheelchair, unable to walk. The specialist working with him remarked privately to Joe's wife that Joe's deterioration was the fastest he'd seen from any disease.

At the end of five years, Jack is still working at health. "It's my full-time job," he jokes. He walks two miles every morning before catching the bus to his office downtown. He says he still can't picture himself in a wheelchair. He also gives speeches at local hospitals and schools. His message?

"Your attitude has an outcome. Focus on the positive."

What Is Attitude?

Attitude.

No other word is more important to people who want to change their lives for the better.

Attitude can be defined as the filter through which an individual sees the world. And although the reality of people, places, things and events in the world remains constant, each of us has an individual *perception* of those people, places, things and events. Our attitude is the filter that colors those perceptions.

Have you ever known someone who was almost always happy and confident? Someone who, even in the face of obstacles or adversity, was able to come out on top by finding the positive aspects of the situation?

How about the opposite kind of person? Have you ever met someone who always seemed to be depressed, angry or cynical? Someone who believed himself or herself to be one of those unfortunates for whom "nothing ever goes right"?

Which one of those people would you rather spend time with? Which one would you be more likely to choose for a trusted friend?

The answer is obvious. People crave the company of others who contribute to their sense of well-being and tend to avoid those who have only depression and negativity to share.

But a positive attitude is not something we are born with. Neither are we born with a negative attitude, incidentally. The development of an individual's attitude takes time and input. Indeed, for most of us, our attitude is now a habit that we've developed over the years.

It's interesting to note that the word "attitude" comes from the same Latin root as the word "aptitude." That root word, aptus, meant "fitness" to the Romans. And indeed, your attitude does have a lot to do with your fitness — physical, mental, emotional, spiritual and even financial fitness.

This handbook will provide some concrete steps you can take to improve your *attitude fitness*. And by improving your attitude, you will discover that you are putting the keys to success in your hands.

Someone once said, "If you think you're a success, you're right. If you think you're a failure, you're right too." The thinking we do about ourselves and about the people, places, things and events of our lives has a definite impact on the way those people, places, things and events *work* in our lives.

This is more than a book about positive thinking. This is a book of positive *actions*. Actions are what change the quality of our lives. If you take the actions suggested in this book, your increased happiness, increased success and increased security are guaranteed.

Your attitude *does* make a difference in the results you get out of life. Think of your attitude as a pair of glasses through which you see the world. Some people wear glasses that make everything blurry; others wear glasses that help them see things more clearly. Some people wear dark, dark, dark sunglasses to block out the brightness of the day, while others wear glasses tinted a light rose color that makes everyone and everything look healthier.

Changing your attitude will probably take time. We suggest that you give yourself thirty days to work with the suggestions in this book. But that doesn't mean that you shouldn't expect to feel a whole lot better, almost immediately. You *will* feel better. And you will be closer to success every day if you work at the ideas in this book.

Make a decision now to choose an attitude that magnifies the positives in your life and diminishes the negatives. If you do, you will have already taken the single most important step toward attitude improvement and success.

The Necessary First Step: Attitude Assessment

What is your attitude today? Do you have a positive, winning attitude that is propelling you toward unlimited success? Or are you like most people? Do you feel that your attitude could stand some adjustment?

On the next page is a short quiz that will help you answer two important questions about your attitude:

1. Is my attitude helping me or hurting me?

2. What particular areas of my attitude need my attention?

Here are the instructions: Answer each question *as quickly as possible*, circling T for true, F for false, and NS for not sure.

Go with your first response. Don't think too much about each statement. Just respond; then move quickly to the next statement.

REMEMBER: Your attitude did not happen overnight. You cultivated it as you experienced the ups and downs of your life. Now it is a habit. Trust your first response to be a genuine indicator of that habit—your present attitude.

An answer key follows the quiz.

Self-test:
What Is My Attitude?

Circle your first response to each statement.

T=True   F=False   NS=Not sure

1. I love waking up in the morning.   T   F   NS

2. I have a goal that is important to me.   T   F   NS

3. Sometimes I get really angry.   T   F   NS

4. It's good to be home.   T   F   NS

5. I'm glad to be alive.   T   F   NS

6. People walk all over me.   T   F   NS

7. I look great today.   T   F   NS

8. I wish I had more friends.   T   F   NS

9. I have enough money.   T   F   NS

10. I love television.   T   F   NS

11. The news depresses me.   T   F   NS

12. Life is good.   T   F   NS

13. Sometimes I'm so happy I cry.   T   F   NS

14. I love trying new things.   T   F   NS

14. trust most people.   T   F   NS

16. I love my job.   T   F   NS

17. I am a disciplined person.   T   F   NS

18. I have a dream.   T   F   NS

19. I'm totally satisfied with my diet.   T   F   NS

20. This test is stupid.   T   F   NS

Answer Key

Total the points indicated for each of the following questions:

Did you finish the test?
    10 points for "Yes"
    0 points for "No"   _____

Did you have fun taking the test?
    10 points for "Yes"
    0 points for "No"   _____

Did you *really* go with your first response
to each question?
    10 points for "Yes"
    0 points for "No"   _____

Are you totally satisfied with your responses
to each of the twenty questions?
    10 points for "Yes"
    0 points for "No"   _____

            TOTAL SCORE   _____

What your score means:
    40   Great! You're definitely on the right track.
    30   Your attitude is probably working against you
          in some situations.
Below 30 Your attitude is hurting your chances for
          success and happiness.

Are you surprised that the scoring for this attitude quiz does not take into account your actual answers to the twenty questions? Here's the reason it doesn't:

How you feel about yourself, your ability to take life lightly and your willingness to keep an open mind are far better indicators of your attitude than any feelings you may have about specific areas of your life.

Certainly, careful study of your responses will give you a good idea of the areas of your life you'd like to change. For example, if you answered Question 4, "It's good to be home," with "false," you may find that you need to work at making your home more pleasant or at finding a new home.

But it is not fair for us (or anyone else) to tell you which answers are "correct" and which ones are "incorrect." What matters most is that your answers work for *you.*

Let's return to the example of "It's good to be home." Maybe you have been sick for the past two weeks and unable to go out. In that case, you might mark that statement "false," but you would have no bad feelings about doing so. You would just be eager to get well so you could spend less time at home.

The same thing holds true for the rest of the statements in the self-test. At first glance, of course, each statement seems to have a "healthy" response and an "unhealthy" one — if you judge yourself by the standards that would work for the majority of people. But what if your case is different?

Consider this Lesson Number One about attitude: No one has the right to tell you how you feel except *you.* You alone are in charge of and responsible for your responses to life. Believing in yourself and trusting your decisions are two excellent ways to build a positive attitude.

Now, what if you answered "no" to any of the four questions on page 9? What does that mean?

If you didn't finish the test, you may want to ask yourself whether you are willing to keep an open mind as you work your way through the rest of this book. Some questions that are asked may seem strange or new to you. But if you're not happy with the outcomes you are experiencing from your present attitude, what have you got to lose? Remember: It is only by giving new ideas and actions a chance that anything ever changes.

If you didn't enjoy yourself while taking the test, you might want to work at developing a sense of humor. The ability to laugh and enjoy the events in one's life is a hallmark of the truly successful individual.

If you didn't write down your first response to any of the twenty questions, it generally indicates one of two things:

1. You were ashamed of your true responses.

2. Someone was looking over your shoulder.

Actually, both of these mean the same thing. For whatever reason, you would rather not let other people know the truth about you. This attitude leads to the need for dishonesty, and its final result is alienation from self. The message you give your heart and brain here is, "There's something wrong with me the way I am."

Imagine how you would feel if everyone you knew told you all day long that there was something wrong with you. Would it make you happy? Of course not. The danger of this mental attitude is obvious.

If you weren't totally satisfied with some of your responses, GREAT! Then you've already identified some of the areas where you need to begin to change. Perhaps you learned that you really love television, and you find yourself a bit ashamed of that. This may be a signal that you believe you spend too much time in front of the TV. What would you rather be doing?

Or maybe you aren't totally happy with your diet. What changes do you want to make? If you take action on the things about yourself that dissatisfy you, your attitude automatically improves. You're telling yourself, "You're valuable to me and I want to make you happy." Imagine how you would feel if *that* is what the people you know said to you all day long. Wouldn't you feel great?

No matter what your responses to any of the questions you've been asked in these pages, the practice at attitude building you get in this book can make a big difference in your life. It is not this book's intention to tell you which beliefs contribute to a positive attitude. That is a personal matter.

Instead, the goal of this book is to give you the tools you need to build the attitude that will make you happy. The only "A+ for Attitude" that exists is in your own heart. If you are truly happy with yourself, if you believe that you can reach your goals and fulfill your dreams, and if you are willing to look for the sunshine behind every black cloud on your horizon ... THEN you will know the glory of a positive, winning attitude.

PART TWO

Building
Your Winning Attitude

The next several pages contain ten Attitude Builders that will help you transform your attitude into the positive, winning one you desire. Part Two is your workbook for attitude improvement. Write on the pages, work with the suggestions presented in them, and participate in the exercises and worksheets they contain.

Here are three reminders before you begin:

1. Set aside a period of time every day for the next thirty days to work with these Attitude Builders. (We have provided a 30-day calendar at the end of this book so that you can schedule the Attitude Builders you will try each day.)

2. Keep an open mind.

3. Try each Attitude Builder at least once. Then, pick and choose the ones that work best for you.

Enjoy yourself, and welcome to a positive, winning attitude.

Schedule Time for Yourself on a Daily, Weekly and Monthly Basis

It's a busy world. Many people these days have appointment books that are bursting their bindings because they are filled with so many commitments, obligations and plans. Perhaps time for yourself is a luxury you feel you just can't afford.

But if you wish to build a positive, winning attitude, the advice is obvious: you *must* find time for yourself. You *must* make yourself a priority.

You are the center of the circle that is your world. No matter how many people, places, things and events are a part of your world, you are still responsible for dealing with them effectively. To be your most capable, you need to be as mentally, emotionally and physically fit as you can possibly be.

Think of your personal effectiveness as a bank account. You can only withdraw that which you have deposited. Take the time, on a daily basis, to deposit thoughts, nurturing experiences, further education or even peace and quiet. You will discover that activities like these renew you and give you the strength you need to remain capable.

For the next thirty days, set aside at least forty-five minutes a day just for you: thirty minutes at the beginning of the day, five minutes during the middle of the day and ten minutes at the end of the day.

Spend your morning time strengthening and preparing yourself for the day ahead. You will find plenty of ideas throughout this book for activities that will help you do this.

Use your midday break to take a time-out to remind yourself of your priorities—

and your strengths. You'll find that five minutes is enough time to step out of the rat race for a moment and recenter yourself.

Before you go to bed, spend ten minutes reminding yourself of the positive events of your day. What did you do that you're really proud of? What good things happened to you? What made you laugh? What made you feel thankful?

So many people are in the habit of doing exactly the opposite. Have you ever lain awake in bed, thinking about all the things you did "wrong" that day? All the things that made you angry or unhappy? And then, have you ever started correcting yourself? "Gee, I SHOULD have done this, I SHOULD have done that ..."

Don't SHOULD on yourself! It's a law of nature that what you keep in your heart and mind is what you will manifest in your life. Focus on the negative and you'll find yourself in a downward spiral of "should haves" and "not good enoughs." Focus on the positive and your life will get better and better.

The time you spend with yourself *daily* for improving your attitude is crucial. But don't stop there. Schedule some time on a weekly and monthly basis also. What things do you do that increase your sense of well-being? Does an afternoon on the golf course relax you? How about a massage? Perhaps you love to read or go to the movies. Many people look forward to classes or seminars.

Use the worksheets on pages 16 and 17 to plan the positive activities in your day, week and month. Time management experts suggest that you plan your day the day before and your week the week before. Then, each morning, review the plans you have made for that day.

If you use a planning calendar of any kind, you may want to keep the information from these worksheets in it. You may also find that copying the 30-day calendar at the end of this book helps you plan your attitude-building activities.

The other nine Attitude Builders in this chapter will help you find additional activities to improve your outlook on yourself and on life. Use the time you set aside for yourself to build your attitude into the positive, winning one you want.

✍ Worksheet #1
A Daily Plan

In the morning

1. What positive activities am I willing to commit to today?

     _____

     _____

     _____

2. Where can I go for five minutes in the middle of my day
    to take a time out? (a car, an empty office, the rest room,
    outdoors, etc.)

     _____

     _____

     _____

At midday

3. What will I do during this midday break to help myself
    stay positive?

     _____

     _____

At the end of the day

4. What am I really proud of today?

     _____

     _____

5. What made me happy today?

     _____

     _____

6. What made me laugh?

     _____

     _____

7. What am I thankful for today?

     _____

     _____

✍ Worksheet #2
Weekly and Monthly Plans

1. What goals do I have for myself this week?

_____

_____

_____

_____

_____

2. What positive actions am I going to take this week?

_____

_____

_____

_____

_____

3. What goals do I have for myself this month?

_____

_____

_____

_____

_____

4. What actions will I take this month to keep myself positively focused?

_____

_____

_____

_____

Make Use of Goal Setting, Affirmations and Visualizations

They work!

It is a proven fact that people who have written goals tend to be more successful throughout their lives than people who do not. Many human potential experts tell the story of a graduation class at Yale that was surveyed in the 1950s. One of the questions in the survey was "Do you have written goals?" Only 3 percent of the class responded "yes." Twenty years later, another survey was taken of those same class members. The 3 percent who had said they did have written goals were outearning the other 97 percent of the class combined.[1]

Goal setting requires that you know what you want, by when you want it and how you'll be able to tell you've achieved it.

An *affirmation* is a positive, results-oriented statement spoken to yourself in the first person. It is stated as if the result you desire is already achieved. Here are some examples:

- I am basking on the beach outside my new home in Laguna Beach.
- I am full of energy at my ideal weight of 125 pounds.
- I am competently handling my responsibilities as Director of Advertising.

A *visualization* is a vivid mental picture of you *in* your affirmation.

The reason that goals, affirmations and visualizations are so powerful is this: Your brain cannot tell the difference between a perceived event, feeling or thought that is real and one that is not. All your brain knows is that it has experienced a perception. If you can effectively visualize yourself already reaching a goal, your brain will begin reprogramming itself for that success.

Another powerful tool is to *act as if.* If you want to weigh 125 pounds someday, visualize yourself at that weight and then *act* that weight. You will be reprogramming your mind to the positive goal, and it will be much easier for your actions to follow suit. When you think of yourself as a thin person, it's easy to act like a thin person. When you think of yourself as a heavy person, every minute of work you do toward being thinner is a fight.

This same principle holds true for any goal you have. Remember: Your present attitude and, therefore, your present outcomes are the results of a habit. It is the program already in operation in your mind that is bringing you the results you see in your life today. Affirmations and visualizations provide your mind with new thought habits. They are a powerful strategy for changing the results in your life.

Affirmations and visualizations can be used for concrete goals, like owning a house on the beach. They are equally powerful for more abstract goals, like wanting to be more trusting of people.

Do your best to put emotion into the affirmations and visualizations you choose for your own success. Emotion supplies an electrical charge to an already powerful technique.

On the following pages you will find worksheets to help you learn the techniques of setting and achieving goals, stating those goals as affirmations and turning those affirmations into powerful visualizations.

> *Happiness is not a goal; it is a by-product.*
> —Eleanor Roosevelt

✍ Worksheet #3
Goal Setting

Part I: Your Goals

On the lines below, write down five of your goals:

Examples:　　I want to be rich.

I want to be thin.

I want to be happy.

1. _____

_____

_____

2. _____

_____

_____

3. _____

_____

_____

4. _____

_____

_____

5. _____

_____

_____

Part II: Making Goals Measurable

Now, make those goals concrete. Do this by stating them in measurable terms. Ask yourself how you will know that you've reached the goal, and you will be well on your way to stating it in measurable terms.

Example: I want to be rich.

How will I know that I am rich?

I will know I'm rich when I earn $150,000 per year and have $25,000 in the bank.

The goal in the previous example needs to be restated as two goals. You should always have one goal statement for each outcome. Therefore, the two restated goals would be:

I want to earn $150,000 per year.

I want to have $25,000 in the bank.

Now it's your turn. Restate in concrete terms the five goals you wrote above. Divide them into more than one goal where necessary. Ask yourself "How will I know that I've achieved this goal?"

1. _____

2. _____

3. _____

4. _____

5. _____

Part III: The Timetable

Now you must decide on your deadlines for achieving these goals. Putting a completion date on your goals lets your mind know that you're serious. It also helps you to plan the actions you need to take.

Reread your goal statements in Part II. Ask yourself of each one: "By when?" Write down your deadlines in the right margin, next to each goal statement.

Example: I want to earn $150,000 per year.

By when? In two years.

Part IV: Making Goals Definite

Go back to your list in Part II again. In every place you have written a desire word like "want" (or "wish" or "hope"), cross it out and replace it with a definite word like "will."

Example: I want to earn $150,000 per year.

I WILL earn $150,000 per year in two years

Part V: Action, Action, Action

Now it's time to chart a road map for achieving your goals. What concrete actions can you take to move yourself closer to the goals you've stated?

Rewrite your goals, with deadlines, on the five numbered lines on page 23. Then, underneath each goal, write down the actions you can take toward achieving that goal.

Finally, choose one action you will take within the next week toward each of your five goals. Be sure to schedule that action on the planning calendar at the end of the book.

Come back to this list weekly and add other actions, always choosing at least one you will take toward each goal in the coming week.

Example: I WILL earn $150,000 per year in two years

Action Steps: I will place an ad for my consulting services in the local papers.

I will write an article about traveling with my children and submit it to three magazines about parenting.

I will work on my novel for three hours per day.

I will check into getting my Ph.D.

GOAL #1: _____
Action Steps:

GOAL #2: _____
Action Steps:

GOAL #3: _____
Action Steps:

GOAL #4: _____
Action Steps:

GOAL #5: _____
Action Steps:

✍ Worksheet #4
Affirmations

Now that you have stated your goals, the next step is to turn them into affirmations. To do this, use the goal statements from Part V of Worksheet 3.

Remember that an affirmation is a positive statement you make to yourself as if the goal has already been realized. Most affirmations start with the words "I am."

Rewrite your five goals from Worksheet 3 as "I am" statements in the numbered spaces below.

1. I am _____

   _____

2. I am _____

   _____

3. I am _____

   _____

4. I am _____

   _____

5. I am _____

   _____

Now, ask yourself how you expect to feel when each of these statements becomes true.

Example: I am earning $150,000 per year.

How does that make me feel? *Proud*

Insert that feeling word into your "I am" statements.

Example: I am proudly earning $150,000 per year.

Your feeling word should not be the same for all of your goals. Also, stay away from words that are overused, like "happy." Find something that can cause an emotional response when you read it aloud.

Rewrite your five affirmations, with the feeling words, here:

1. _____

_____

2. _____

_____

3. _____

_____

4. _____

_____

5. _____

_____

Keep a copy of this list with you in your planning calendar, purse or briefcase so that you can consult it any time you begin to have doubts about your abilities. Recite these statements (even quietly to yourself, if necessary) for a few minutes. CONCENTRATE on what they say. If you do this for three or four minutes, you will find yourself renewed, ready to move ahead with stronger resolve.

Remember: Your brain can't tell the difference between what it is perceiving from the world out there and the world inside. If you make a habit of programming your mind with this positive material, the older negative material will eventually lose its hold on you.

✍ Worksheet #5
Visualizations

Use this checklist for turning your affirmations into visualizations. Remember that to use a visualization means to experience the reality of an affirmation with as many senses as possible, as if it were already true.

You may wish to make an audio recording of these points to aid you while you have your eyes closed. Be sure to speak slowly and gently, and give yourself plenty of time to follow each direction.

- Choose an affirmation to work with

- Read that affirmation aloud, slowly, five times. Carefully digest each word.

- Close your eyes

- Concentrate on *seeing* your affirmation

  —What does it look like?

  —Is it a photograph, a painting or a movie?

  —Where are you?

  —Is it bright or dark?

  —What are you wearing?

     What colors?

     Any design on the material?

     Shoes?

     Hairstyle?

  —What details are in the background of the picture?

  —Is anyone else there?

- Most likely, you are seeing this picture as though you are looking at yourself from outside the picture. Now, move yourself into the image you see of yourself, so that you end up looking out of the eyes of the "you" in the picture.

- Now, listen to the sounds in your picture.

    —What noises are associated with what you're doing?

    —Are they loud or soft?

    —Is there music? What kind?

    —Are there any background noises?

- What other sensations are you experiencing?

    —Is it cold or hot or just right?

    —Can you feel the texture of your clothes?

    —What can you feel of your environment?

    What are you standing on?

    Wood?

    Linoleum?

    The ground?

    —What can you smell?

- You now have a complete mental image of that which you desire. Concentrate on it for the next three or four minutes. Make it as real as possible for yourself. Really FEEL it.

- Now, repeat your affirmation to yourself once more, while you are in this picture

- Finally, open your eyes

Keep a Positive Focus

How we each react to the world is the result of a habit—a way of thinking we've each established over the years of our lives. To keep a positive focus is to break a habit. It may take a lot of work in the beginning, but it provides a huge reward.

Have you ever thought to yourself "I should stop being so negative"? The first thing wrong with that type of thinking, of course, is that it has "should" in it. People don't respond well to "should" statements because they come from a basis of shame. It's hard to feel like you're worthwhile enough to change things for the better when you're operating from a basis of shame.

But there's a second error in the statement. Have you ever tried to *stop* doing something? Perhaps you stopped smoking, or stopped overeating, or stopped getting to work late. But have you ever stopped *thinking* in a certain manner?

Stopping a behavior is often difficult. Stopping a thought process is practically impossible. When you stop something, you leave a void. And that void acts like a vacuum, trying to suck back in anything it can. This is one reason that many smokers find they gain weight when they quit smoking. That void is at work filling itself with something else—in this case, food. But there is a better way:

- Don't try to STOP thinking in a certain way
- START thinking in another way
- Don't say to yourself, "I shouldn't think that way."
- Say instead, "What positive action can I take right now to make myself feel better?"

28

If you get into the habit of replacing your negative thoughts with positive ones, eventually that habit will stick. The positive thoughts will actually crowd out the negative ones—there will simply be no more room for them.

Experiment with diminishing the negatives in your life by magnifying the positives. It's the old "is this glass half-empty or half-full" question. Harbor in your heart the good feelings you have; let the painful ones roll off your back.

Indeed, the best way to maintain a positive focus is to fill your day with positive actions. They will keep you busy, and often they will provide you with positive feedback from the world.

Page 30 contains a checklist of positive actions you can use to get started. Add your own ideas to the bottom of the list. Work to accomplish at least three of them a day.

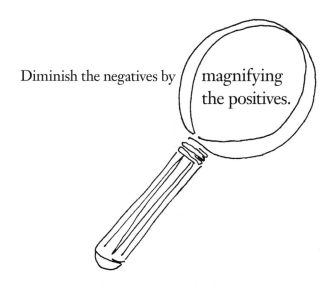

Diminish the negatives by magnifying the positives.

✍ Worksheet #6
Positive Action Checklist

- Write a thank-you note
- Call a friend
- Donate money anonymously
- Take the dog for an extra-long run
- Send flowers
- Invite a friend for dinner
- Bake a cake for the office
- Buy a pound of gourmet coffee for the office coffee pot
- Donate some old books to the library
- Give some toys to a children's home
- Take your neighbor's garbage to the curb while you're taking your own
- Call your parents
- Volunteer to work for a local charity
- Do someone else's chore
- Fingerpaint with your kids
- Write a love letter
- Your own ideas:

  _____

  _____

  _____

  _____

Take Excellent Care of Your Physical Self

There are three areas related to your physical self that need to be addressed when you are working to improve your overall attitude:

- Diet

- Exercise

- Nurturing

Diet

What you choose to put into your body is your business.

There are hundreds of health and diet books espousing different philosophies about what you need to eat (and not eat) for peak performance and great health. But in the end, it is *you* who must be able to live with your dietary choices.

The best way to decide whether your diet is helping you or hurting you is to keep a Food and Feelings Log for a week. Use it to record everything you eat, the time you eat it and how much of it you eat.

But don't stop there. Once an hour, take a couple of seconds to jot down your mental and emotional state at that moment.

At the end of the week, take a look at your log. Look especially for the feeling you are hoping to reduce: sadness, anxiety or any others. Can you see any patterns that tie back to the food you ate half an hour or more *before* you experienced the feeling? For example, many people notice a correlation between coffee and anxiety or between sugar and depression.

A sample log sheet is provided on page 34. The information you glean from studying your emotional responses to the food you eat will help you decide which step to take next. It may be as

31

simple as switching to decaffeinated coffee. Indeed, your next step could also be to pick up a diet or health book. But at least you will have based that decision on your own situation.

You see, a key component of a positive, winning attitude is the ability to trust your own judgment about yourself *first*. You don't need to assume that any "expert" knows more about your inner workings than you do. Certainly, outside sources can provide you with valuable information that is appropriate to your needs. Just don't let other people tell you what your needs are. YOU are the expert on that.

Exercise

If you are already involved in a regular exercise program, you know how much good physical effort can do for your attitude.

The next time you are very angry or depressed, really *exert* yourself physically. Push yourself to the limit of your endurance by running, bike riding or doing aerobics or any other activity. Exhaust yourself. You'll be amazed at how effectively your anger or depression is flushed from your system.

To find a good exercise program, do what's just a little uncomfortable for you. Don't push yourself beyond your ability, but remember that one of the goals of exercise is to increase your heart rate. You will have to go one or two steps further than would normally be comfortable for you.

If you haven't exercised for quite a while, don't rent an exercise video and expect to keep up with it! Start small. Maybe even just ten sit-ups and ten toe touches every morning for a few weeks is enough. Develop the *habit* of exercise first, and then gradually increase your endurance.

Nurturing

If you are like most adults, nurturing is the area of your physical care that is probably suffering the worst neglect. You must take the time to nurture yourself physically. Every once in a while, you need to slow down enough to savor a sensory experience.

Do you usually have precious little time for your meals and, therefore, eat quickly without really tasting what you're eating? Slow down occasionally. Take an hour to eat dinner! And make it a very special meal, with lots of different tastes and textures.

Do you usually drive too fast through the countryside on your way to work? Get up an hour early someday, and take the time to pull off the road and walk in a meadow. Enjoy the sights, sounds and smells.

Another area sorely suffering in most adults' lives is the area of nurturing physical contact. Virginia Satir, an expert psychologist, has what she calls a daily hug prescription:[2]

DAILY: 4 hugs for survival
          8 hugs for maintenance
          12 hugs for growth

Researchers have discovered that hugging can help you live longer, protect you against illness, cure depression, alleviate stress, strengthen family relationships and help you get to sleep at night without medication. Think of what it can do for your attitude!

Most adults have a taboo against touching people they are not intimate with—except for a handshake or pat on the back. Start hugging in a place that feels safe to you, perhaps with a very close friend. But DO start hugging.

Other suggestions for nurturing your physical self are found on page 36, along with space for you to record some of your own ideas. Make sure to build some of them into your weekly attitude-building strategy.

> *The mind is the limit—*
> *it's not the body.*
> —Arnold Schwarzenegger

✍ Worksheet #7
Food and Feelings Log
Example

Time	Food	Feeling
7 A.M.	coffee coffee orange juice	tired
8 A.M.	coffee 2 glazed donuts coffee	wired
9 A.M.		tired
10 A.M.	diet cola small bag potato chips	sluggish, but anxious
11 A.M.		sluggish
12 NOON	tuna sandwich whole wheat bread, apple celery and carrots, diet cola	tired
1 P.M.		happy, strong
2 P.M.	4 chocolate cookies	efficient, clearheaded
3 P.M.		wired
4 P.M.		tired
5 P.M.	coffee coffee	wired
6 P.M.		tired
7 P.M.	2 glasses red wine steak, baked potato salad bar, white bread	mellow, satisfied
8 P.M.	strawberry ice cream	stuffed, tired
9 P.M.		tired
10 P.M.	diet cola popcorn w/butter and salt	
11 P.M.		wired

✍ Worksheet #7
Food and Feelings Log

Time	Food	Feeling
7 A.M.		
8 A.M.		
9 A.M.		
10 A.M.		
11 A.M.		
12 NOON		
1 P.M.		
2 P.M.		
3 P.M.		
4 P.M.		
5 P.M.		
6 P.M.		
7 P.M.		
8 P.M.		
9 P.M.		
10 P.M.		
11 P.M.		

✍ Worksheet #8
Nurturing Your Physical Self

- Take a leisurely bath by candlelight
- Lie in the grass on a sunny day
- Get some hugs
- Walk in the rain
- Get a massage
- Have your hair professionally shampooed
- Make snow angels
- Jump in a pile of leaves
- Have a tender afternoon with someone special
- Get some more hugs
- Sit in a hot tub
- Get a manicure *and* a pedicure
- Take a nap
- Arrange for an elegant meal and spend an hour eating it
- Listen to your very favorite music for an hour
- Go to a museum
- Wear your formal clothes for an afternoon
- My ideas:

_____

_____

_____

_____

Make Lemonade
From the Lemons in Your Life

There are many people who believe that the world is out to get them. Don't let yourself slip into that lie!

The world is NOT out to get you. In fact, a good case can be made for the premise that the world is out to do you good.

Become, as self-esteem expert Jack Canfield calls it, an inverse paranoid.[3] Make lemonade from the lemons in your life.

Search for the positives in every situation. No matter how bleak things *appear* to be, keep searching until you find the hidden benefits. You WILL find them.

Experts in Neuro-Linguistic Programming (NLP) refer to this process as *reframing*.[4] It actually means to see an event from a different perspective: a perspective that is to your own advantage. Indeed, it is very much the same as making lemonade from the lemons in your life.

Worksheet 9, on the next page, shows how this process works.

✍ Worksheet #9
Lemons Into Lemonade

Lemon	Lemonade
• I was just robbed. My entire paycheck was taken — in cash.	The person who took it must have really needed it. Maybe my house insurance covers it.
• I lost my job.	GREAT! Now I can find something I really like.
• This restaurant doesn't serve my favorite dish— after we drove for an hour and a half just to get here!	I've always wondered what Sesame Tangerine Beef tastes like. And what a nice talk we had in the car!

NOW, YOU TRY:

My husband (or wife) left me!   _____

_____

_____

I was just passed over for the promotion they promised me!   _____

_____

_____

The bank denied our loan.   _____

_____

_____

TRY MAKING LEMONADE FROM SOME OF YOUR OWN LEMONS:

Lemon	Lemonade
_____	_____
_____	_____
_____	_____
_____	_____
_____	_____
_____	_____
_____	_____
_____	_____
_____	_____
_____	_____
_____	_____
_____	_____
_____	_____
_____	_____
_____	_____

Build a Support Group

No human being can survive in a vacuum.

All of our lives are dependent, to some extent, on other people. There is no such thing as total self-sufficiency. Each of us must rely on others to help us meet some of our needs and reach some of our goals.

Imagine what life would be like if each of us were an island, responsible for procuring our own food, making our own clothing and finding suitable shelter. Possibly, we could *survive* this way. But most likely we would be living in caves, eating roots and berries and wearing fig leaves—hardly a life of quality.

So, certainly, we need each other just to have supermarkets where we can purchase a wide variety of foods. We need each other so we can shop for clothing of all styles, situations and climates. And we need each other to build and furnish our homes, condominiums and apartment buildings.

But these are only our most basic material needs. Human beings also have great needs for affiliation, for meaningful relationships and for self-actualization. In short, we need to *belong*: people who understand us; friends who offer a shoulder to lean on; fellow human beings who share with us their problems and solutions, their hopes and their dreams—these are the contacts that all of us need to survive in a sometimes troubling world.

Build your support group with friends, family members, coworkers, heroes and others with whom you have something in common. You need to be able to turn to these people for encouragement, understanding, love and emotional support. Many times these people will also be able to educate and inspire you. Perhaps they can help you find new solutions to old problems. Or maybe they can help you stay motivated through a difficult task.

Much business literature today is filled with the advice to "Go forth and network." But the word "network" sounds just a bit too impersonal. Wouldn't it be better to "Go forth and make friends"?

There are many formal support groups in just about every location across the United States. Church groups, parent groups, 12-step programs and organizations for people dealing with any number of life situations are in abundance nationwide. These groups can be a valuable resource to anyone wanting to improve his or her attitude: one of the keys to feeling better about any situation you find yourself in is to find some other people in the same situation. Then, you can share your feelings and hopes with each other.

But you must go further.

To develop a positive, winning attitude, you must have a *personal* support group. You must have a group of people that you trust and respect—a group of people that you are willing to stick by in good times and in bad.

It is recommended that you have at least five close friends at all times. Carry their phone numbers with you always. Better yet, memorize them. When you find your attitude plummeting, make a phone call. If the first person is not available, call the second. Keep dialing until someone answers, and then share your feelings. Let your friend remind you of the good things about you and help you find the good things about your situation.

It's important to remember that the purpose of a support group is to share *strengths*. Avoid using your friends just for complaining. Focus on the positive. Never forget: That in which you invest your time and energy increases. You cannot afford to give power to whining and complaining.

On the next page is a worksheet that will help you see the possibilities in your own neighborhood. Remember: a formal support group is great. But you need to take it further. Start building your personal support group today.

> *Fortunate are the people whose roots are deep.*
> —Agnes Meyer

✍ Worksheet #10
Finding Support

Where to Look

- At the office
  - — Committees
  - — Unions
  - — Professional societies
  - — Work groups
  - — Teams
- Church groups
- Parent/Teacher groups
- Neighborhood groups
- Evening classes at a local college
- Self-help organizations
  - — Weight Watchers
  - — Alcoholics Anonymous
  - — Narcotics Anonymous
  - — Overeaters Anonymous
  - — Adult Children of Alcoholics
  - — Co-Dependents Anonymous
  - — Local hospital's wellness classes
  - — Parenting classes
- Singles groups
- Political groups
- Seminars and lectures
- Library programs
- Museum programs

Keep a Log of
Your Victories and Gratitudes

If you keep a list of the victories, successes and gratitudes in your life, you will greatly improve your attitude.

Here's why:

You have already learned in this book that the thoughts you spend time thinking are the ones you give power to. If you avoid negative thoughts by replacing them with positive ones, you will gradually change your mental habit from a damaging one to a productive one.

Also, the list that you keep will be a permanent record you can refer to any time you need to remind yourself of how wonderful you and the world really are.

The best place to keep this list is in a special journal. Buy yourself a beautiful notebook or diary. Then, discipline yourself to write in it every night for a few moments before you retire. Work at it. Find at least three victories and three gratitudes every day. Before you know it, in just thirty days, you will have close to two hundred positive entries recorded in your personal victory book.

A *victory* is any success you've had that day—large or small. Here are some examples:

- Finished letter to mother
- Called Mary Lou and volunteered to help with office party
- Ran three miles this morning
- Ate only half of my dessert tonight
- Waxed car
- Let my husband win at chess even though I love to beat him

A *gratitude* is something that happened in your day that you are thankful for, something that you appreciate. A gratitude doesn't need to be tied to someone you would personally thank. Just stay with the events in your day that made you feel good. Here are some examples of gratitudes:

- I thought I was going to be late for my meeting with a client, but it turned out he got stuck in the same traffic jam I did.
- The soup of the day was my favorite—beef vegetable.
- I got a letter from my best friend.
- I drove a friend home from work and had to take a different route home. I found out later there was a terrible accident on my regular route—at the exact time I'm usually in that spot.

Developing a sense of your own accomplishments and fostering in yourself an attitude of gratitude are excellent ways to engender a positive attitude.

Can you find three things about yourself to be proud of every day? Can you find three things you're grateful for?

These two questions are vitally important to developing a winning outlook on life. Remember that the items you list don't need to be major events. Every positive you can think of is significant.

Worksheet 11, on the next page, lists some questions to help you get started identifying your victories and your gratitudes. Don't give up. Write them down every night for at least thirty days. At the end of that time, you will be feeling so good you won't want to stop.

If you develop the habit of finding the positives in every day, you will be replacing the negative, downward spiral of a bad attitude with the concrete proof that yes, good things DO happen—often. You will never again be able to whine to yourself, "Things NEVER go my way."

> *Each day provides its own gifts.*
> —Ruth P. Freedman

✍ Worksheet #11
Victory and Gratitude Checklist

Ask yourself the following questions to help find the victories and gratitudes in your day.

1. What did I do today that I'm proud of? _____

   _____

   _____

2. Did I complete anything today? _____

   _____

   _____

3. Did I do something I was anxious about? _____

   _____

   _____

4. Did I keep a promise? _____

   _____

   _____

5. Did I do anything I've been meaning to do for a long time? _____

   _____

   _____

6. Did I make any decisions today that will improve the quality of my life? _____

_____

_____

7. Did I laugh today? At what? _____

_____

_____

8. Did I spend any time with people I love? _____

_____

_____

9. What unexpected events came my way? _____

_____

_____

10. Did I help anyone today? _____

_____

_____

11. Did anyone help me? _____

_____

_____

Put Your
Positive Attitude Into Action

Have you ever heard the ancient law of karma? What goes around comes around. You're going to reap just what you sow. You need to give to get.

There are probably hundreds of variations in the wording, but they all translate to mean the same thing. *What you do to and for others tends to come back to you.* And there most certainly is a breathtaking joy in giving.

Look for ways to share your positive attitude by doing kind things for others. There are three good reasons to do this:

1. By doing "good deeds," you demonstrate to yourself that there is enough kindness in you to go around. Most prosperity experts claim that if you give away a percentage of your income, you will help yourself get richer because you will be *acting as if* you are a philanthropist. The same is true for simple kindnesses. If you give away some of your good feelings, you will be reinforcing to yourself their abundance.

2. By helping other people and by doing kind things for them, you will often receive positive feedback as a natural consequence. And, of course, positive feedback *does* make most of us feel pretty good.

3. Finally, the time you spend performing kind acts is time that you will no longer have available to spend on negative thinking. You will be reprogramming your mind just by spending your time differently.

One more important note: If good deeds make you feel good, try doing some *anonymously.* There is an absolute thrill in sitting back and claiming no credit for an act that has made someone else's day a little brighter or someone else's life a little easier.

Acting out your positive attitude is really nothing more than passing along the gratitude you have for the good things in your life. Sometimes you will even find great ideas for kind acts in the list of gratitudes you prepare every night. (See Attitude Builder #7.)

Plan some positive actions in advance every day. Try to do at least one anonymous kindness each day. When you plan your day, make a special point of listing a couple of your "good deed ideas" for that day. Another benefit you will find as you begin to put your positive attitude into action is that your new outlook on life is contagious. Most people notice that as their attitudes improve, their environments also improve.

> *Patience is needed with everyone,*
> *but first of all with ourselves.*
>
> —Francis de Sales

✍ Worksheet #12
Positive Action Plan

Here are some examples of ways to put your positive attitude into action:

- Play with the neighbor's dog for a few minutes on your way into the house at night

- Send a funny card to a coworker who helped you out with a project—even if it was part of her job. (Send the card to her work address—what a pleasant surprise it is to get a handwritten note amid the pile of "Dear Sir," "To Whom It May Concern," and otherwise less-than-inspiring business mail.)

- Water and tend to the office plants after work hours one day

HERE ARE SOME OF MY OWN IDEAS:

_____

_____

_____

_____

_____

_____

_____

_____

_____

_____

_____

Know Your Strengths

Know your strengths. . . *and focus on them*. Sure, we all have weaknesses. But we all have strengths also. Never forget that *what you focus on in your mind is what you give your power to.*

Isn't it better to give power to the great things about you?

Take a minute right now to list ten of your strengths on the lines below:

_____   _____

_____   _____

_____   _____

_____   _____

_____   _____

Could you do it? How long did it take you? Or did you get stuck after writing down four or five items?

Most people DO get stuck with this list. Many of us have been educated to "be humble," to not brag about ourselves. Too many of us have taken that advice from our childhood to heart— to the point of never acknowledging our own strengths or greatness.

If you had trouble with this list, ask some of your friends and family members for help. Ask them what they see as your strengths.

And don't forget to tell them what you see as their strengths too. It's so easy for us to fall into the habit of commenting only on what needs work in our friends and family members' characters. But again, this process gives strength to those deficiencies. Have you ever been in the position of "falling out of love" with someone? Dwelling on the other person's deficiencies is exactly how it happens! If we focus on the negative for long enough, eventually we have a hard time even *remembering* the positive.

Make a determined effort to turn this process around, in dealing both with yourself AND with others. Find the great things about yourself and about your friends and family members at every turn. And then pat yourself (and them) on the back.

A checklist of strengths is found on page 52 in Worksheet 13. Use it to find the great things about you and about the people you love.

> *A great obstacle to happiness is*
> *to expect too much happiness.*
> —Fontenelle

✍ Worksheet #13
Strengths Checklist[5]

Place a check mark next to each strength you think you have. To share this list with others, ask them to place a check mark next to each strength they think you have. Then place a check mark next to each of the strengths you think they have.

__ able	__ dedicated
__ affectionate	__ dependable
__ appreciative	__ diligent
__ articulate	__ disciplined
__ artistic	__ eager
__ assertive	__ effective
__ athletic	__ efficient
__ attractive	__ elegant
__ brave	__ encouraging
__ bright	__ excited about life
__ businesslike	__ fair
__ calm	__ feeling
__ candid	__ forceful
__ caring	__ frank
__ clean	__ friendly
__ committed	__ funny
__ common sense	__ generous
__ communicates well	__ gentle
__ compassionate	__ good cook
__ considerate	__ good friend
__ cooperative	__ good listener
__ courteous	__ good parent
__ creative	__ graceful
__ daring	__ grateful

___ happy   ___ physically fit
___ hard worker ___ pleasant
___ healthy   ___ positive
___ helpful   ___ quick learner
___ honest   ___ resilient
___ humorous   ___ respectful
___ independent ___ responsible
___ inspiring   ___ risk-taker
___ intelligent   ___ self-reliant
___ joyful   ___ self-confident
___ kind   ___ sense of humor
___ leader   ___ sensitive
___ lovable   ___ spiritual
___ loving   ___ spontaneous
___ loyal   ___ straightforward
___ mathematical ___ strong
___ mechanical   ___ team player
___ motivates others ___ tolerant
___ musical   ___ trusting
___ natural   ___ truthful
___ observant   ___ understanding
___ orderly   ___ unselfish
___ organized   ___ visionary
___ open   ___ warm
___ patient   ___ well-dressed
___ peaceful

Please add any other strengths you have that are not listed here:

_____

_____

Tap Your Inner Power

At one time or another, probably everyone of us has felt a certain inner strength come to our aid at the very moment we needed it most. It is often in a crisis situation that we find ourselves surprised at the results we are able to achieve.

In his book *Peak Performance*, Charles Garfield tells the story of a grandmother in Florida who single-handedly lifted an automobile off the ground so her grandson could be pulled out from underneath it. In fact, Mr. Garfield's entire book is concerned with the kind of inner power that makes a feat like that possible.

Remember the savings account analogy we used in Attitude Builder #1? Think of your inner power as a savings account. The more you deposit into it, the more you will have available when you need to withdraw from it. Many truly successful and happy people have found that they can gain control over their store of inner power—they can make it available at will, not just in crises. Imagine how much better you would feel if you knew you had the power to overcome any difficulty you might encounter. Wouldn't that make you feel more confident about taking risks, about facing difficulties?

Certainly, no one can meet every single one of life's challenges with that much power or that much confidence: this is just one of the facts that makes us all human. But we can improve our odds.

There are six basic techniques for building and using your inner power:

1. Maintain a sense of wonder
2. Retreat and recharge

3. Feel deserving

4. Give freely

5. Strive for balance

6. Be yourself

Maintain a Sense of Wonder

The best way on earth to rediscover your sense of wonder is to spend a day with a preschool child. Watch how children get excited about the smallest things!

As we grow out of childhood, we so often grow out of our sense of wonder as well. We look up to the adults around us and notice that they are more "dignified." Wishing to emulate them, we tone down our own childlike response to life. It's as if we subconsciously tell ourselves to "be cool."

Yet, in many ways, it is our sense of wonder that gives our inner power the fuel it needs to burn brightly. Take some time now to reclaim yours. Make an agreement with a good friend that you will go somewhere neither of you has been before (anywhere will do—from a meadow to a mall) and use all of your senses to discover it. Really notice what's going on around you.

Keeping track of the people, places and events in your life that make you feel grateful or lucky is another wonderful way to stay in touch with your sense of wonder. (This technique has already been discussed in Attitude Builder #7.)

Retreat and Recharge

We are living in a very busy world. Most of us are faced with many daily demands on our time and energy—and often those demands conflict with each other. But biologists claim that there is only so much information or stimulation an organism can effectively process before it is simply unable to process any more.

The need for occasional retreat is a basic fact of life.

There are many different ways to retreat and recharge.

Getting a good night's sleep is one of the most basic methods. But there are many others:

- Go for a drive alone
- Listen to some soothing music
- Take yourself on a date—a nice dinner and a movie
- Do relaxation exercises
- Lose yourself in visualization
- Take a walk or go for a swim
- Read something inspirational
- Lie in the sun

It doesn't matter so much *what* you do to relax—just *that* you do it. Schedule downtime into your life. Don't wait until you "have the time." Even if you have only fifteen minutes a day, you will find that your relaxation time pays a huge dividend: renewed power.

Feel Deserving

There are two basic ways to feel deserving:

- Live a life that makes you proud
- Reinforce yourself

Much of this book has dealt with living a life that makes you proud. If you follow your heart, you will find yourself a much happier and more fulfilled person. But often just a few moments of reinforcement can greatly magnify your feelings of "deservability."

Worksheet 14 is a simple exercise guaranteed to make you feel like a million dollars — just by making you feel that you DO deserve it all. The theory that makes this technique so successful isn't difficult to understand: Sometimes we fail to achieve the goals we desire because subconsciously we don't feel ourselves to be worthy of them. By turning that undeserving thought around, we free ourselves—and our inner power—to work fully.

✍ Worksheet #14
I Deserve It All

1. Think of something you really, really want.

   Example: I really want to be a great painter.

2. Put that desire into this statement:

   I, _____(your name)_____ , deserve it all. I deserve
   _____(your desire)_____ .

   Example: I, Tyler Ross, deserve it all. I deserve to be a
   great painter.

3. Think of something else you really, really want.

   Example: I really want to have a home on the lake.

4. Add that desire to your statement from #2.

   I, _____(your name)_____ , deserve it all. I deserve
   __(desire #1)__ AND __(desire #2)__ .

5. Repeat this process until you have ten desires worked
   into your "I deserve it all" statement. But remember to
   add those desires one at a time. It will help you to focus
   your desires if you say the statement aloud to yourself
   each time you add a desire. Or, if you think you have
   the time, you can *write* out your desire statements as you
   think of each desire. By both writing them and speaking
   them, you will give yourself the benefit of installing
   them into your psyche on more than one level. You will
   be using your hand to write, your eyes to read, your
   voice to speak and your ears to hear.

6. Enjoy the burst of power you feel! That is the energy—
   the inner power—that is available to help you reach
   your dreams.

Give Freely

There are many adages based on the advice to give freely. Perhaps you've heard some of them:

- "You reap what you sow."
- "To give is better than to receive."
- The Golden Rule—Do unto others as you would have them do unto you

Indeed, the act of giving does increase your inner power. When you give, you remind yourself that you do have enough to give. And if you have enough to give, then you certainly have enough for yourself. You feel prosperous. And that feeling of prosperity generates more prosperity.

It is important to remember that prosperity is a term that applies to much more than money: If you give love freely, you will feel lovable. If you give your time freely, you will feel like you have enough time. If you give some smiles freely, you will feel like smiling.

Get in the habit of giving, with no expectations of return. You will be amazed at how much *is* returned.

Strive for Balance

We are all multifaceted people. It is important to spend some quality time devoted to each facet, or we may find our inner power withering.

Identify the things that are important to you—the things that are an integral part of who you are. Then make sure to focus some energy on each one every week.

A common problem for many of us is to think that the means to our priorities are the priorities themselves. Is the job the priority, or is the income from it the priority? Are evening classes the priority, or is the degree that will make you more marketable the priority? When we see our TRUE priorities, we often find ways to save ourselves time and trouble.

Worksheet 15 is to help you establish a balance among your many activities. Work through it carefully to discover the best balance for you.

> *Too many people miss the silver lining because they're expecting gold.*
>
> —Maurice Seitter

✍ Worksheet #15
My Personal Balance

EXAMPLE

My name ___*Kyle Andrews*___

What is important to me? (List as many items as you find.)

My children, Randy and Ellen

My income—to provide the life we want

My marriage—Kelly

Horseback riding

Learning about business—so I can start my own company

Gardening

Now, use the chart on the next page to list the number of waking hours per week you spend on various activities. Include all the items you listed above, but also include the other things you do with your time: commuting, eating, watching TV, etc. Include an "Other" category for activities that are not particularly time-consuming or important.

Activity	Time Spent Per Week
- *My job (income)*	*40 hrs.*
- *Commuting*	*10 hrs.*
+ *Quality time w/Randy & Ellen*	*20 hrs.*
++ *Quality time w/Kelly*	*Shame on me! Only 2 hours??*
+ *Horseback riding*	*For as rarely as I ride, the weekly time is less than 1 hr!*
+ *Reading business books*	*10 hrs.*
+ *Gardening*	*4 hrs.*
Eating	*15 hrs.*
TV	*6 hrs.*
Meetings	*3 hrs.*
Other (shopping, phone calls, etc.)	*15 hrs.*

Now, place a plus sign in front of each item that you wish you could spend MORE time on.

Place a minus sign in front of each item that you wish you could spend LESS time on.

Use the pie chart below to record your IDEAL balance. Remember to leave a wedge of the pie for your miscellaneous and unavoidable activities.

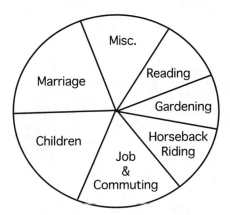

Now, consider your options. Spend as much time as you need to find creative solutions, but make sure that you find enough time for EVERY item you have marked with a plus sign.

1. *I could buy books on tape and listen to them while commuting.*

2. *Kelly and I could garden and ride horses together. Also, we could eat out once a week.*

3. *The time I save listening to books can be spent actually beginning my own business!!*

4. *I guess I need to accept the fact that I am in a transitional phase. Until my business is up and running, I just need to realize it's like working 2 jobs.*

5. *Because I am in transition, I need to look at this again next month.*

Remember: Your store of inner power is like a savings account. You MUST make regular deposits in order to enjoy the security of a large available balance. Spending time on the things you consider to be a part of you is one of the best ways to increase your account.

✍ Worksheet #15
My Personal Balance

My name _____

What is important to me? (List as many items as you can think of.)

_____

_____

_____

_____

_____

_____

_____

_____

_____

_____

_____

_____

_____

_____

Now, use the chart on the next page to list the number of waking hours per week you spend on various activities. Include all the items you listed above, but also include the other things you do with your time: commuting, eating, watching TV and so forth. Include an "Other" category for activities that are not particularly time-consuming or important.

Activity	Time Spent Per Week

Now, place a plus sign (+) in front of each item that you wish you could spend MORE time on.

Place a minus sign (-) in front of each item that you wish you could spend LESS time on.

Use the pie chart below to record your IDEAL balance. Remember to leave a wedge of the pie for your miscellaneous and unavoidable activities.

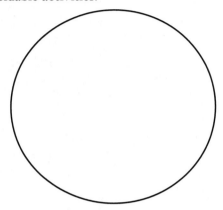

Now, consider your options. Spend as much time as you need to find creative solutions, but make sure that you find enough time for EVERY item you have marked with a plus sign.

_____

_____

_____

_____

_____

_____

_____

Remember: Your store of inner power is like a savings account. You MUST make regular deposits in order to enjoy the security of a large available balance. Spending time on the things you consider to be a part of you is one of the best ways to increase your account.

Be Yourself

Of course! As you have worked your way through this book, you have probably noticed your sense of yourself and of your power growing. Certainly you have found some ways to help yourself to a better attitude.

But never forget that you are a human being—a unique human being. There is no reason to feel that you should be happy all the time, or that you should even be working at being happy every time that you're not. The human experience is one of varying levels of energy and emotion.

Have you ever had a day when you just felt bad and you didn't even want to feel better? Have you ever had a day when you just felt like staying in bed and watching old movies on TV—and you did?

We must look at ourselves realistically—and give ourselves permission to be less than perfect. Don't worry about those occasional feeling-poor days. As a matter of fact, plan for them now. Accept the fact that no matter how hard you work at it, there is bound to be a morning when you wake up and say, "No. Not today." The next day just pick up where you left off.

> *Be not afraid of growing slowly, be afraid only of standing still.*
> —Chinese proverb

PART THREE

Maintaining Your Winning Attitude

So you have now been practicing the ten Attitude Builders on the preceding pages for thirty days. How do you feel? Do you feel energetic and joyful? Do you feel like a winner?

How do you maintain this positive, winning attitude?

The answer is simple: Practice, practice, practice. Keep at it! Keep working with the attitude-building principles contained in this book and on any others you've discovered yourself.

Plan your attitude-building and attitude-maintaining activities on a daily, weekly and monthly basis. Schedule them just as you schedule your other important tasks.

Use a planning calendar like the one at the end of this book or one that you have already been using.

Don't let yourself backslide. Maintaining your winning attitude requires a continued effort. You didn't adopt your less positive, less winning attitude overnight. It took years to develop. Until you practice your new attitude for a few years, you can't be sure that it will truly become a habit for you.

Sure, this requires effort. But by now, you must be convinced of how valuable that effort is. The rewards you reap with a positive, winning attitude are immeasurable. Your world is now at your command; you no longer need to be at the command of your world.

You've learned that your mental attitude *does* correlate to the results you achieve in life. And you've seen that your expectations of life tend to be realized—whatever they are, positive or negative.

You've learned that your attitude is indeed tied closely to its root—fitness. Your attitude *does* determine your fitness to deal with the people, places, things and events of your life.

So don't stop now. Keep reaching. Keep growing.

As you use the calendar at the end of this book, map your weekly and monthly attitude strategies in addition to your daily strategy. Plan your day the day before—plan your week the week before.

Don't be afraid to break new ground, to try something not in this book. There is no limit to the positive, life-affirming activities available to you. Use your own creative ideas and share them with others.

You are now well on your way to a lifetime of success and unlimited possibility. It's all in your hands!

> *The longer I live, the more beautiful life becomes.*
> —Frank Lloyd Wright

Your Career

Are you happy with your career? Or do you tend to think of it as "just my job"?

There's no reason you can't enjoy your job. In fact, there is at least one excellent reason *to* enjoy it: Most people spend more of their waking hours at their jobs than anywhere else!

How sad it must be to not enjoy such a large portion of one's life.

Once you begin building your positive, winning attitude, it's likely you will be willing to do whatever needs to be done to provide yourself with the highest possible level of job satisfaction.

If you already love your job and you see your career heading in exactly the right direction, GREAT!

If you aren't so satisfied, consider your options:

- Changing your job, or

- Changing your attitude about your job

By now you know that complaining just doesn't do much good. Avail yourself of the resources at your disposal and take action.

Perhaps you should look for a new job, or continue your education. Maybe a trip to the library and a look at books about career success will help. Do you have some friends or contacts that could help point the way to better opportunities? Have you really decided what it is that your heart is aching to do? How can you turn that desire into real employment?

Or maybe it is just an attitude adjustment that you need. What are the positive things about your present job? How can it lead you to the career end you desire? Spend some time thinking about how to most effectively refocus yourself to accomplish what you want.

Ultimately, we are each responsible for the happiness and satisfaction we glean from life. We must each take the responsibility for making ourselves true winners at life.

Relationships

Accentuate the positive.

That is the universal advice counselors, clergy and relationship experts give about the matter of human relationships.

It seems that the more intimate we are with people, the easier it is to dwell on their shortcomings.

In order to be truly happy in a relationship, however, it is exactly the opposite habit we need to form.

Search for the beauty in your friends and loved ones. As you remind them of their strengths, you will be reminding yourself of them as well. Turn around that pair of glasses that seems to magnify every fault, so it makes those faults smaller. Magnify the good points instead.

Remember that relationships are not like a jigsaw puzzle: Two half-people don't make one whole-people. You are a complete person, with or without intimate relationships in your life. And, of course, it's not realistic to expect that some other person can do it for you. NO ONE can make you feel better about YOU.

The world is set up so that each human being, ultimately, is responsible for being a whole and complete person on his or her own. We must work at loving ourselves, no matter how many others love us or not. When you love yourself, all else follows.

Certainly, by maintaining a positive, grateful attitude, you will be very appealing to other positive, grateful people. And those are exactly the kinds of friends who will help you be all that you wish to be.

Don't be surprised if some of your negative friends or acquaintances don't seem to enjoy your company quite as much as they once did. Like tends to attract like. Invite your friends to join you in your effort to build a positive, winning attitude. But if they don't, remember that there are plenty of others out there waiting—you just haven't met them yet.

When you trust and believe in yourself, the world is your oyster. And by the time you have finished working with the Attitude Builders in this book, trusting and believing in yourself will be just *one* of the valuable tools at your fingertips.

' *The most thoroughly wasted of all days is that on which one has not laughed.*

—Chamfort '

A Life of Quality

The way that you look at yourself and your world has a powerful effect on every area of your life. Your career and your relationships are two areas that are bound to improve as your attitude improves. But that is only the beginning.

Your attitude also affects your health, your happiness, your ability to acquire money, the likelihood that you will reach your goals, even the quality of your fondest dreams.

When you have an attitude of "I'm worth it!" you'll find that you are willing to do whatever is necessary to improve the quality of your life—because now you believe that you deserve only the best.

There are hundreds of books, audiocassettes and videos available that can help you improve the quality of your health, your finances, your ability to reach goals, your career and your relationships. When you are uncomfortable with yourself in any area, seek the help you need.

Life is a process of continual growth. Growth comes about when we effectively meet the challenges in our lives. Think of the challenges you face in just that way. The next time you're faced with a situation that looks difficult, tell yourself: "GREAT! Now, I can grow!"

The truth of the human condition is that very few of us choose to grow just for the heck of it. Pain forces us into it.

You DO have the power to achieve anything you want out of this life. You have the potential for unlimited happiness and opportunity. And when life looks tough, just remember that a diamond is only a lump of coal that made the best of a little pressure.

PART FOUR

Putting It All Together: What You Look Like as a Winner

Give this book an honest thirty days of effort. Don't give up on yourself, no matter what. Accept that you will never be perfect, but that you will be better ... and better ... and better ... and better.

When you bought this book, did you have a picture in your mind of what you'd be like with a more positive, winning attitude? Are you closer to that image of yourself than you were thirty days ago? Of course you are!

Keep at it. Assess your attitude every thirty days for the rest of your life. Make any adjustments that you need to and keep on growing in your capacity for happiness.

Finally, remember the three most important questions you can ever ask of yourself to judge whether your attitude is helping you or hurting you:

1. Am I enjoying myself?

2. Do I feel shameless?

3. Have I answered questions 1 and 2 honestly?

Happy growing. Remember that your masterpiece won't be finished until you draw your last breath. The possibilities for success in your life are unlimited. Michelangelo's motto was "I'm still learning."

Acknowledge yourself for not quitting. Congratulate yourself for still learning. And prepare yourself for the fabulous results of your positive, winning attitude.

MONTHLY PLANNING CALENDAR

Use this calendar to schedule the Attitude Builders you will try this month.

Fill in the dates to correspond to the month for which you are scheduling activities.

Sunday	Monday	Tuesday	Wednesday	Thursday	Friday	Saturday

Notes

1. Anthony Robbins, *Unlimited Power* (Chicago: Simon & Schuster Audio Publishing Division, 1986), Audiotapes.

2. Virginia Satir, *Self-Esteem I: The Loving and Empowering Yourself Seminar* (Culver City, CA: Self-Esteem Seminars, 1990), 13.

3. Jack Canfield, *How to Build High Self-Esteem* (Chicago: Nightingale-Conant, 1988), Audiotapes.

4. Bandler, Grinder, and Andreas, *Frogs into Princes* (Moab, UT: Real People Press, 1979), 137.

5. Jack Canfield, adapted from *Self-Esteem I: The Loving and Empowering Yourself Seminar* (Culver City, CA : Self-Esteem Seminars, 1990), 55-57.

Available From SkillPath Publications

Self-study Sourcebooks

Climbing the Corporate Ladder: What You Need to Know and Do to Be a Promotable Person by Barbara Pachter and Marjorie Brody

Coping With Supervisory Nightmares: 12 Common Nightmares of Leadership and What You Can Do About Them by Michael and Deborah Singer Dobson

Defeating Procrastination: 52 Fail-Safe Tips for Keeping Time on Your Side by Marlene Caroselli, Ed.D.

Discovering Your Purpose by Ivy Haley

Going for the Gold: Winning the Gold Medal for Financial Independence by Lesley D. Bissett, CFP

Having Something to Say When You Have to Say Something: The Art of Organizing Your Presentation by Randy Horn

Info-Flood: How to Swim in a Sea of Information Without Going Under by Marlene Caroselli, Ed.D.

The Innovative Secretary by Marlene Caroselli, Ed.D.

Letters & Memos: Just Like That! by Dave Davies

Mastering the Art of Communication: Your Keys to Developing a More Effective Personal Style by Michelle Fairfield Poley

Organized for Success! 95 Tips for Taking Control of Your Time, Your Space, and Your Life by Nanci McGraw

A Passion to Lead! How to Develop Your Natural Leadership Ability by Michael Plumstead

P.E.R.S.U.A.D.E.: Communication Strategies That Move People to Action by Marlene Caroselli, Ed.D.

Productivity Power: 250 Great Ideas for Being More Productive by Jim Temme

Promoting Yourself: 50 Ways to Increase Your Prestige, Power, and Paycheck by Marlene Caroselli, Ed.D.

Risk-Taking: 50 Ways to Turn Risks Into Rewards by Marlene Caroselli, Ed.D. and David Harris

Speak Up and Stand Out: How to Make Effective Presentations by Nanci McGraw

Stress Control: How You Can Find Relief From Life's Daily Stress by Steve Bell

The Technical Writer's Guide by Robert McGraw

Total Quality Customer Service: How to Make It Your Way of Life by Jim Temme

Write It Right! A Guide for Clear and Correct Writing by Richard Andersen and Helene Hinis

Your Total Communication Image by Janet Signe Olson, Ph.D.

Handbooks

The ABC's of Empowered Teams: Building Blocks for Success by Mark Towers

For more information, call 1-800-873-7545.

Notes

Notes

Notes

Notes

Notes

Notes